The English Sound System

an innovative guide

packaging

This book describes how we produce sounds in English:

How we produce sounds in English can be described in terms of a series of guidelines. We can group these guidelines together into **packages**:

package:	pausing
guidelines:	We usually pause for a short period between sentences.
	We also pause for a longer period when we are thinking of something to say.

package:	blending
guidelines:	Each sound blends into both the preceding and following sound.
	We blend everything we say into a single flow of sounds.
	We sometimes blend the w and y sounds so much it's hard to distinguish them.

This book describes 17 of these packages. The names of packages all end in *ing*. The following is a list of all the packages in this book, including the page number each package starts on:

To use an analogy from programming languages, the names of packages are our "reserved words". These words—together with their derived words—are all the terminology you will need to describe any feature of English pronunciation:

sounding	*sound*
marking	*mark*
shortening	*shortened*

However, this book describes a very specific feature (the sound system) of the entire English language system. It therefore relies on some terminology that is used in traditional grammar ("verbs", "nouns", etc)—although you will most likely already be familiar with this terminology. If you would like to learn a complete system for analyzing ALL features of the English language without any prior knowledge, you can find a simple and elegant system of language analysis in my six-volume *englishing* series, an innovative and comprehensive guide to the grammar of English. So, if you like the system used in this book, be sure to check out the main series!

englishing

level one

You should read through this book from the first page to the last page, working through each package in sequence. This book is essentially a coursebook—anything that is introduced is based on what has gone before. At no point will you need to skip ahead to read about a particular point. However, once you have read through the book, you can then think of the book more as a reference guide since, for the most part, all the particular features of any given topic are described together.

> In those cases where something is introduced briefly before it is properly described, I have highlighted this by means of a box—like this.

Throughout this book, there are a lot of examples to illustrate the features described. If there is a * symbol before an example, this means that no-one would ever say that example normally:

1

* Another teabag need I.
I need another teabag.

* Him took me to Florence for my birthday.
He took me to Florence for my birthday.

If there is a ? symbol before an example, this means that most people would usually avoid saying that example—typically because it would sound unnatural:

2

? My mother and she used to work together.
Her and my mother used to work together.

? We could grab a coffee first? —Yes, we could grab a coffee first.
We could grab a coffee first? —Yes, we could.

Almost all the examples in this book have an accompanying audio. These audios can be downloaded absolutely free from **tinyurl.com/dpdrfyck**. Alternatively, If you would like me to email you the audios instead, simply contact me at **david.young@email.com**. The number for each audio file is given next to each example:

the z sound

With the z sound, the tip of the tongue comes close to but does not touch the ridge just above the top front teeth:

7

zone	freezer	has
zown	friyzər	haz

You have just completed your first package—congratulations! You are now ready to proceed to the next. I hope you find this book useful and interesting. I would be very happy to hear any feedback, comments or questions you have online.

David Young

sounding

We use the organs in our body (the mouth, vocal cords, lungs, etc) to produce different **sounds**. There are 16 basic sounds in English. These can all be defined by how we position our lips, teeth and tongue. We can represent these sounds with the following marks:

b   w   v   ð   d   l   z   r   y   g   i   e   a   ə   o   u

> Marks are symbols we use to represent English graphically. In all of the examples in this book, marks in *this font* indicate how we write that example. Marks in this font indicate how we pronounce that example:
>
> | | |
> |---|---|
> | *example* | how we write |
> | egzampəl | how we pronounce |
>
> Marks are described later in this book. Until then, when you come to an example, you should focus only on how we pronounce that example.

With some sounds, parts of the mouth come together to close off the stream of air escaping from the mouth. With other sounds, no parts of the mouth come together—the stream of air escaping from the mouth is largely uninterrupted. We can therefore divide sounds into two groups—closed sounds and open sounds:

b   w   v   ð   d   l   z   r   y   g   closed sounds

i   e   a   ə   o   u   open sounds

closed sounds

When we produce closed sounds, parts of the mouth come together to close off the stream of air escaping from the mouth. Closed sounds differ according to which part of the mouth—the lips, teeth, tongue and back of the mouth—touches which other part of the mouth.

The b sound

With the b sound, the top and bottom lips touch each other:

1

barn	*number*	*cab*
barn	nəmbər	khab

the w sound

With the w sound, the lips are rounded (as when we say *boo*, *food*, *who*, etc). Instead of the top and bottom lips touching each other, it's almost as if the left and right corners of the lips try to touch each other:

2

win	*fewer*	*low*
win	fyuwər	low

the v sound

With the v sound, the top front teeth touch the bottom lip:

3

van	*level*	*of*
van	levəL	ov

the ð sound

With the ð sound, the tip of the tongue touches the top front teeth and the bottom front teeth touch the underside of the tongue:

4

this	*other*	*bathe*
ðis	əðər	beyð

the d sound

With the d sound, the tip of the tongue touches where the top front teeth meet the gums:

5

day	*leader*	*mad*
dey	liydər	mad

the l sound

With the l sound, the tip of the tongue touches the ridge just above the top front teeth—but then the sides of the tongue drop in order to let air pass on both sides:

6

love	*feeling*	*yellow*
ləv	fiylin	yelow

the z sound

With the z sound, the tip of the tongue comes close to but does not touch the ridge just above the top front teeth:

7

zone	*freezer*	*has*
zown	friyzər	haz

the r sound

With the r sound, the tip of the tongue comes close to but does not touch the flat area above this ridge:

8

red	*carry*	*feature*
red	khari	fiytyər

the y sound

With the y sound, the upper side of the tongue comes close to but does not touch this flat area:

9

yellow	*fire*	*say*
yelow	fayər	sey

the g sound

With the g sound, the back of the tongue touches the back of the mouth:

10

garden	*forget*	*fog*
gardən	fərgit	fog

open sounds

When we produce open sounds, no parts of the mouth come together—the stream of air escaping from the mouth is largely uninterrupted. Open sounds differ according to the vertical and horizontal position of the tongue in the mouth. Horizontally, the tongue might be positioned toward the teeth or toward the back of the mouth. Vertically, the tongue might be positioned toward the roof of the mouth or it might be lying flat in the mouth. In addition, the lips may be rounded.

the i sound

With the i sound, the tongue is positioned horizontally toward the teeth and vertically toward the roof of the mouth:

11

ill	*fig*	*busy*
iL	fig	bizi

the e sound

With the e sound, the tongue is positioned horizontally toward the teeth and vertically in a central position:

12

elder	*beg*	*said*
eLdər	beg	sed

the a sound

With the a sound, the tongue is positioned horizontally in a central position and vertically lying flat in the mouth:

13

add	*car*	*hack*
ad	khar	hak

the ə sound

With the ə sound, the tongue is positioned both horizontally and vertically in a central position:

14

other	*fever*	*Hannah*
əðər	fiyvər	hanə

the o sound

With the o sound, the tongue is positioned horizontally toward the back of the mouth and vertically in a central position. The lips are also rounded:

15

odd	*Thor*	*saw*
od	þor	so

the u sound

With the u sound, the tongue is positioned horizontally toward the back of the mouth and vertically toward the roof of the mouth. The lips are also rounded. This sound usually (but not always) occurs before a w sound:

16

ooze	*would*	*few*
uwz	wud	fyuw

whispering

Imagine that you ask someone what sound a bee makes. They will make a buzzing sound:

zzzzzzzzzzzz…

Now, imagine that you ask someone what sound a snake makes. They will make a hissing sound:

sssssssssssss…

This hissing sound is exactly the same as the buzzing sound—the position of the lips, teeth and tongue teeth is the same. The only difference is that, with the hissing sound, we don't vibrate our vocal cords—we essentially **whisper** the sound. We can whisper all the closed sounds and all the open sounds. By doing so, we essentially double the number of sounds we use in English:

b	w	v	ð	d	l	z	r	y	g	closed sounds
p	ʌ	f	þ	t	ʃ	s	ɹ	ħ	k	whispered closed sounds

i	e	a	ə	o	u		open sounds
hi	he	ha	hə	ho	hu		whispered open sounds

whispering closed sounds

We can whisper all the closed sounds.

whispering the b sound

If we whisper the b sound, we get the p sound:

3

bat	*ribbon*	*robe*
bat	ribən	rowb
pat	*Ripon*	*rope*
phat	ripən	rowp

whispering the w sound

If we whisper the w sound, we get the ʌ sound. This sound only usually occurs after a t or k sound:

4

went	*wine*	*wash*
went	wayn	wosy
twenty	*twine*	*quash*
tʌenti	tʌayn	kʌosy

whispering the v sound

If we whisper the v sound, we get the f sound:

5

veer	*rival*	*leave*
viyər	rayvəL	liyv
fear	*rifle*	*leaf*
fiyər	rayfəL	liyf

whispering the ð sound

If we whisper the ð sound, we get the þ sound:

6

fathom	*either*	*within*
faðəm	iyðər	wiðin
thumb	*ether*	*pith*
þəm	iyþər	piþ

whispering the d sound

If we whisper the d sound, we get the t sound:

7

dime	*medal*	*raid*
daym	medəL	reyd
time	*metal*	*rate*
thaym	metəL	reyt

whispering the l sound

If we whisper the l sound, we get the ɬ sound. This sound only usually occurs after a p or k sound:

8

leads	*loud*	*lie*
liydz	lawd	lay
pleads	*cloud*	*apply*
pɬiydz	kɬawd	əpɬay

whispering the z sound

If we whisper the z sound, we get the s sound:

9

zoo	*lazy*	*knees*
zuw	Leyzi	niyz

Sue	*Lacey*	*niece*
suw	Leysi	niys

whispering the r sound

If we whisper the r sound, we get the ɹ sound. This sound only usually occurs after a p, t or k sound:

10

ray	*reason*	*rude*
rey	riyzən	ruwd
pray	*treason*	*crude*
pɹey	tɹiyzən	kɹuwd

whispering the y sound

If we whisper the y sound, we get the ɦ sound. This sound only usually occurs before uw:

11

you	*you'd*	*use*
yuw	yuwd	yuwz
hue	*queued*	*pews*
ɦuw	kɦuwd	pɦuwz

whispering the g sound

If we whisper the g sound, we get the k sound:

12

guard	*bagging*	*log*
gard	bagiŋ	log
card	*backing*	*lock*
khard	bakiŋ	lok

whispering open sounds

We can also whisper all the open sounds. However, we only usually whisper the beginning of an open sound before pronouncing the rest of the sound as normal. We can represent this by putting the mark h before the open sound:

13

ear	*Ellen*	*eye*
iyər	elən	ay
here	*Helen*	*high*
hiyər	helən	hay
earl	*order*	*oops*
ərL	ordər	uwps
hurl	*hoarder*	*hoops*
hərL	hordər	huwps

nasalizing

Say *maybe* repeatedly:

1

> *maybe, maybe, maybe, maybe, ...*

Then, suddenly grab your nostrils so you close off the stream of air escaping from the nose. You should immediately hear *baby*:

2

> *..., maybe, maybe, baby, baby, ...*

The first sound in *maybe* and *baby* is exactly the same—the position of the lips, teeth and tongue is the same. The only difference is that, with *baby*, we're not letting the stream of air escape from the nose. With *maybe*, we are letting the stream of air escape from the nose—we essentially **nasalize** the sound. We can nasalize three closed sounds and all the open sounds. Again, by doing so, we essentially increase the number of sounds we use in English:

b	w	v	ð	d	l	z	r	y	g	closed sounds
m	-	-	-	n	-	-	-	-	ŋ	nasalized closed sounds

i	e	a	ə	o	u	open sounds
ï	ë	ä	ə̈	ö	ü	nasalized open sounds

nasalizing closed sounds

We can nasalize the b, d and g sounds.

nasalizing the b sound

If we nasalize the b sound, we get the m sound:

3

bad	*elbow*	*dub*
bad	elbow	dəb
mad	*Elmo*	*dumb*
mad	elmow	dəm

nasalizing the d sound

If we nasalize the d sound, we get the n sound:

4

dice	*trader*	*head*
days	tɪeydə	hed
nice	*trainer*	*hen*
nays	tɪeynə	hen

nasalizing the g sound

If we nasalize the g sound, we get the ŋ sound:

5

logging	*sag*	*rig*
lOgiŋ	sag	Rig
longing	*sang*	*ring*
lOŋiŋ	saŋ	Riŋ

nasalizing open sounds

We can also nasalize all the open sounds. However, we only usually nasalize an open sound when it is followed by a nasalized closed sound. We can represent this by putting the mark ¨ above the open sound:

6

sit	*fed*	*gag*
sit	fed	gag
sin	*fen*	*gang*
sïn	fën	gäŋ
cub	*cog*	*would*
kəb	kOg	Vud
come	*Kong*	*woman*
käm	kÖŋ	Vümän

Nasalizing open sounds can probably best be analyzed as a natural consequence of the open sound being followed by a nasalized closed sound. Therefore, for convenience, I have not used the mark ¨ elsewhere in this book.

blending

When we speak, we say one sound after another so that each sound **blends** into both the preceding sound and the following sound:

r	a	s	y		rasy	*rash*
k	hi	t	ə	n	khitən	*kitten*
a	ŋ	g	l	o w	aŋglow	*Anglo*

We blend everything we say into a single flow of sounds:

Are you looking forward to the new movie?
aryuwlukiŋforwərdtəðənuwmuwvi

How are you doing today?
hawaryuwduwiŋtədey

We sometimes blend the w and y sounds so much that it's hard to distinguish them. We do this when they follow certain other sounds. Note the pronunciation of y after the following closed sounds:

	joke	*manager*	*merge*
d	dyowk	manədyər	mərdy
	casual	*treasure*	*vision*
z	khazyuwəL	tɹezyər	vizyən

Note also the pronunciation of w and y after the following open sounds:

4

	email	meme	see
i	iymeyL	miym	siy
	ape	base	say
e	eyp	beys	sey
	hour	doubt	wow
a	awər	dawt	waw
	eye	light	sky
a	ay	layt	skay
	owner	voter	go
o	ownər	vowdər	gow
	oil	soil	annoy
o	oyəL	soyəL	ənoy
	doom	loose	glue
u	duwm	luws	gluw

The same blending occurs if the above closed and open sounds are whispered:

5

	chalk	kitchen	catch
t	tyok	khityin	khaty
	shy	mission	wish
s	syay	misyən	wisy
	heat	team	key
hi	hiyt	thiym	khiy
	haze	tape	pay
he	heyz	theyp	phey
	house	pout	cow
ha	haws	phawt	khaw
	haiku	kite	tie
ha	haykuw	khayt	thay

	hone	*toad*	*Poe*
ho	hown	thowd	phow
	hoist	*toys*	*coy*
ho	hoyst	thoyz	khoy
	hoodoo	*pool*	*too*
hu	huwduw	phuwL	thuw

With closed sounds, the same blending also occurs between words:

6

	red	*yams*	*red yams*
d	red	yamz	redyamz
	put	*yes*	*Put "yes".*
t	phut	yes	phutyes
	is	*yellow*	*This is yellow.*
z	iz	yelow	ðis izyelow
	kiss	*you*	*I wanna kiss you.*
s	khis	yuw	awonəkisyuw

marking

We can represent speech graphically using symbols:

three
þriy
3

happy
hapi
:)

sound marks

Sound marks represent sounds. The full set of sound marks are:

b	w	v	ð	d	l	z	r	y	g	-	i	e	a	ə	o	u
p	ʌ	f	þ	t	ʃ	s	ɿ	ħ	k	h	-	-	-	-	-	-
m	-	-	-	n	-	-	-	-	ŋ	¨						
-	-	-	-	ʔ	-	-	-	-	-							
-	-	-	-	ɔ	-	-	H	-	-							
-	-	V	-	D	L	-	R	-	-	-	-	-	A	-	O	-
-	-	-	-	T	Γ	-	Я	-	-	-	-	-	-	-	-	-

> The last four rows of sound marks are more complex and so are described later in this book.

script marks

We only use sound marks in resources like this book, where we need to represent the sounds of English fairly accurately. Everywhere else, we use script marks to represent sounds. The full set of script marks are:

a b c d e f g h i j k l m n o p q r s t u v w x y z

Script marks represent the same sounds as their equivalent sound marks:

1

bin	*flow*	*help*
bin	flow	heLp
red	*worn*	*Zak*
red	worn	zak

However, in English, script marks represent sounds pretty loosely. For example, some script marks don't have an equivalent sound mark:

2

canteen	*fox*	*jam*
kanthiyn	foks	dyam
nice	*queen*	*Xerxes*
nays	kʌiyn	zərksiyz

Some sound marks don't have an equivalent script mark:

3

bang	*father*	*math*
baŋ	faðər	maþ
plank	*puke*	*try*
pɫaŋk	pʰuwk	tɪay

A single script mark can represent several different sounds:

4

sad	*vision*	*has*
sad	vizyən	haz
axe	*made*	*Russia*
aks	meyd	rəsyə

A single sound can be represented by several different script marks:

5

photo	*office*	*cough*
fowdow	ofis	khof

all	*roars*	*law*
oL	rorz	lo

Therefore, in English, it's almost easier to think of script marks and the sounds they try to represent as two entirely different and almost unrelated things—almost like Chinese logograms or Egyptian hieroglyphs:

晚		*night*
ài	grḥ	nay?

> There are, however, some patterns that can help us pronounce script marks. These are described later in this book.

There is, however, a major advantage of script marks in English representing sounds pretty loosely. Although it is more difficult at first to learn which script marks represent any given word, once we have learned this, we can differentiate words that sound the same much more easily:

6

aisle	*isle*	*I'll*
ayəL	ayəL	ayəL

buy	*by*	*bye*
bay	bay	bay

pausing

When we speak, we blend everything we say into a single flow of sounds:

1

She messaged me on Facebook.
syimesidydmiyonfeysbuk

What's your name?
wotsyorneym

However, sometimes we **pause**. For example, we usually pause (for a short period) between sentences. We can represent this by using spacing with sound marks:

2

She messaged me on Facebook but... I'm not gonna respond.
syimesidydmiyonfeysbukbə? aymnoʔgonərisphond

What's your name? Where do you come from?
wotsyorneym werdəyəkhəmfrom

We also pause (for a longer period) when we are thinking of something to say:

3

Her number was... 6379... 13... I think.
hərnəmbərwoz siksþriysevənayn wənþriy ayþiŋk

Let's have... David on reception.
letshavə deyvidonrisepsyən

shortening

We often pronounce a sound **shorter** than its surrounding sounds. We can represent this by using a smaller version of the sound mark:

1

| *add* | *loo* | *melds* |
| ad | luw | melDz |

| *at* | *loose* | *melts* |
| at | luws | melTs |

We do this when an open sound appears before a whispered sound in the same word:

2

| *cup* | *ridges* | *wedding* |
| kəp | Ridyiz | Vediŋ |

| *cub* | *riches* | *wetting* |
| kəb | rityiz | Vetiŋ |

If there is a closed sound between the two, we also shorten that:

3

| *go* | *knees* | *send* |
| gow | niyz | send |

| *goat* | *niece* | *sent* |
| gowt | niys | sent |

Elsewhere in this book, I have not usually indicated shortened sounds.

lengthening

We often pronounce a sound **longer** than its surrounding sounds. We can represent this by using a bigger version of the sound mark:

1

criminal	*Jessica*	*this season*
kɹ**i**minal	dy**e**sika	ði**S**iyzən

We can lengthen both open sounds and closed sounds:

2

began	*murder*	*information*
big**a**n	m**ə**rda	infoHm**e**ysyən
have various	*see your*	*who would*
ha**V**eriyəs	si**y**oH	hu**W**ud

Elsewhere in this book, I have not usually indicated lengthened sounds.

lengthening open sounds

When a word contains two or more open sounds, we lengthen one of those sounds:

3

a lot of	*character*	*warrior*
el**O**tOv	k**ha**rakta	w**O**riyə

In this case, we also pronounce the sound slightly louder:

4

a few	Dubai	zoology
efyUw	dubAy	zuwOlowdyi

We usually lengthen the first open sound in any given word:

5

birthday	didn't	lots of
bƏHþdey	dIdənt	lOtsOv

However, with many words, we lengthen a different open sound:

6

computer	inside of	technique
kOmpħUwta	insAydOv	teknIyk

Therefore, when we learn a new word that contains two or more open sounds, we also have to learn which open sound we lengthen:

7

arrow	democracy	see you later
Arow	demOkrasi	siyuwlEytə

lengthening closed sounds

When a word ending in a closed sound is followed by a word beginning with the same closed sound, we usually pronounce those sounds as one and lengthen the resulting sound:

8

fantastic	cake	a fantastic cake
fanthastik	kheyk	eifanthastiKheyk
why	you	why you
way	yuw	waYuw

We also sometimes do this with certain words made of two separate components:

9

mis...	spell	misspell
mis	spew	miSpew
room	mate	roommate
ruwm	meyt	ruwMeyt

weakening

We often pronounce a sound **weaker** than usual. When we do so, we pronounce that sound less prominently:

battle	*his*	*what*
batəL	hiz	wȮt
battle	*his*	*what*
baɔəL	iz	wɔʔ

We can weaken the t sound:

get	*little*	*must*
get	litəL	məst
get	*little*	*must*
geʔ	liɔəL	məs

We can weaken whole words:

he	*into*	*will*
hiy	intuw	wil
he	*into*	*will*
hi	intə	əL

If we can weaken, we usually do weaken to some extent. Not weakening at all would often sound fairly unnatural:

4

We should put it in front of the yacht.
? wiysyudputitinfrəntOvðəyOt
wisyədpuʔiɔinfrənʔəðəyOʔ

What are you getting at?
? wOtaHyuwgetiŋat
wOɔəyuwgeɔiŋaʔ

weakening the t sound

There are three ways we weaken the t sound.

pronouncing the t sound normally

We can pronounce the t sound normally. In this case, the tip of the tongue touches where the top front teeth meet the gums. However, the tongue then stays there—we don't "release" the t sound. We can represent this by using the sound mark ? instead of t:

5

a bit	*not*	*write*
əbit	nOt	rayt
a bit	*not*	*write*
əbiʔ	nOʔ	rayʔ

We usually do this with any t sound at the end of a word—especially when it is the last sound we say:

6

art	*bit*	*cat*
aHt	bit	khat
art	*bit*	*cat*
aHʔ	biʔ	khaʔ

pronouncing the t sound differently

When can pronounce the t sound differently. In this case, no parts of the mouth come together to close off the stream of air. Instead, the throat comes together to close off the stream of air—almost as if we were pausing for an extremely short period. We can represent this by using the sound mark ɔ instead of t:

7

a lot of	*computer*	*department*
əlOtOv	kəmpʰuwtə	dipʰaHtmənt

a lot of	*computer*	*department*
əlOɔOv	kəmpʰuwɔə	dipʰaHɔmən?

We don't usually do this with a t sound at the beginning of a word or before a r or y sound in the same word:

8

thirteen	*met Rick*	*sit you*
þəHɔiyn	meɔrik	siɔuw

teen	*metric*	*situ*
tiyn	metrik	sityuw

not pronouncing the t sound at all

Sometimes, we weaken the t sound so much that we don't pronounce it at all. We can represent this by not using a sound mark at all:

9

best eat	*ghost*	*oldest aunt*
bestiyt	gowst	OLdistaHnt

best go	*Ghostbusters*	*oldest one*
besgow	gowsbəstəz	OLdiswən

We usually do this when a word ending in st is followed by a closed sound:

10

fast	*forward*	*fast forward*
fAst	fowəd	fAsfowəd

tallest	*boy*	*the tallest boy*
tholist	boy	ðətholisboy

weakening whole words

When we weaken a whole word, we pronounce certain sounds in that word less prominently:

11

and	*him*	*she*
and	him	syiy

and	*him*	*she*
ən	im	syi

For example, we often pronounce an open sound as ə or de-whisper that open sound—or both:

12

are	*her*	*have*
aH	həH	hav

are	*her*	*have*
ə	əH	əv

We often don't pronounce certain closed sounds at all:

13

a	*ourselves*	*would*
ey	awəseLvz	wud

a	*ourselves*	*would*
ə	aHseLvz	əd

We only weaken certain words—though all of these are very common words. The following are some of the more common:

14

a	ey	ə
am	am	əm
an	an	ən
and	and	ən
are	aH	ə
as	az	əz
at	at	ət, aʔ, ə

be	biy	bi
can	khan	kən
could	khud	kəd
do	duw	də
for	foH	fəH, fə
from	frOm	frəm
had	had	həd, əd
has	haz	həz, əz
have	hav	həv, əv
he	hiy	hi, i
her	həH	əH
here	hiyə	iyə
hers	həHz	əHz
herself	həHself	əHself
him	him	im
himself	himself	imself
his	hiz	iz
I	ay	ə
into	intuw	intə, inɔə
me	miy	mi
of	Ov	əv, ə
our	awə	aH
ours	awəz	aHz
ourselves	awəseLvz	aHseLvz
shall	syaL	syəL
she	syiy	syi
should	syud	syəd
than	ðan	ðən
that	ðat	ðət, ðəʔ
them	ðem	ðəm
themselves	ðemseLvs	ðəmseLvz
to	thuw	tə, ɔə
was	wOz	wəz
what	wOt	wət, wOʔ, wə
we	wiy	wi
will	wil	wəL, əL

would	wud	wəd, əd
you	yuw	yə
you're	yoH	yə
your	yoH	yə
yourself	yoHself	yəself
yourselves	yoHseLvz	yəseLvz

We don't usually weaken a word if it's the last word we say:

15

I won't be there but some of my friends will.
? aywown?biðeH bətsəməmayfrendzəL
aywown?biðeH bətsəməvmayfrendzwil

Who are you talking to? —You!
* huwəyətokiɳtuw   yə
huwəyətokiɳtuw   yuw

strengthening

We often pronounce a sound **stronger** than usual. When we do so, we pronounce that sound more prominently. We can represent this by using an even bigger version of the sound mark:

1

| *Kyle* | *lots* | *tomorrow* |
| kayəL | lOts | təmORow |

| *Kyle* | *lots* | *tomorrow* |
| k**a**yəL | l**O**ts | təm**O**Row |

As with lengthening, we pronounce a strengthened open sound longer and louder than its surrounding sounds—but to an even greater extent than with lengthening:

2

| *Costa* | *seen* | *took* |
| kOsta | siyn | thuk |

| *Costa* | *seen* | *took* |
| k**O**sta | s**i**yn | th**u**k |

We only strengthen open sounds—and we only usually strengthen one open sound in any word. When the word contains one open sound, we strengthen that:

3

| *not* | *she* | *Val* |
| nOt | syiy | vaL |

| *not* | *she* | *Val* |
| n**O**t | sy**i**y | v**a**L |

When the word contains two or more open sounds, we strengthen the lengthened one:

4

in case	Peter	regular
iŋk**e**ys	p**i**ytəR	R**e**gyələR

in case	Peter	regular
iŋk**e**ys	p**i**ytəR	R**e**gyələR

We strengthen in order to clarify or emphasize a word:

5

I'm not gonna call her anymore.
amnO?gənəkoləHenimoH

I'm not gonna TEXT her anymore... but I might email.
amnO?gənət**e**kstəHenimoH bə?aymayɔiymeyl

Many items are for sale today.
meniyaytəmzaHfoHseyLtədey

MANY items are for sale today... but this one isn't.
m**e**niyaytəmzaHfoHseyLtədey bəɔðiswənizənt

We often do this to contradict someone:

6

Aren't I on lates next week?
aRəntayOnleytsneks?wiyk

Aren't I on LATES next week? (You seem to think I'm on early shift.)
aRəntayOnl**e**yts nekstwiyk

My brother was not at that bar at that time.
maybRəðəRwOznO?atðə?baRa?ðataym

My brother was NOT at that bar at that time. (Someone said he was.)
maybRəðəRwOzn**O**t atðə?baRa?ðataym

Strengthening also allows us to indicate a range of different meanings without changing words:

7

Tom was at the party.
tOmwOzaʔðəpaRti

TOM was at the party. (You seem to think it was someone else.)
t**O**m wOzaʔðəpaRti

Tom WAS at the party. (You seem to think he wasn't.)
tOmw**O**z aʔðəpaRti

Tom was at the PARTY. (You seem to think he was somewhere else.)
tOmwOzaʔðəp**ɑ**Rti

We won't attend the conference next week.
wiwownʔətendðəkOnfəRənsnekstwiyk

We won't ATTEND the conference next week... but we will view it online.
wiwownʔət**e**nd ðəkOnfəRənsnekstwiyk bəʔwiwiLvyuwiʔOnlayn

We won't attend the CONFERENCE next week... but we will attend the plenary.
wiwownʔətendðək**O**nfəRənsnekstwiyk bəʔwiwilətendðəpliynəRi

We won't attend the conference NEXT week... but we will do the week after.
wiwownʔətendðəkOnfəRənsn**e**kstwiyk bəʔwiwiLduwðəwiykAftəR

We sometimes pause for a short period immediately after a word that contains a strengthened sound:

8

I have never seen that guy before.
ayəfnevəRsiynðaʔgaybifoR

I have NEVER seen that guy before.
ayəfn**e**vəR siynðaʔgaybifoR

She uploaded it here.
syiyəplowdidithiyəR

She uploaded it HERE not there.
syiyəplowdidit**hi**yəR noʔðeR

Elsewhere in this book, I have not usually indicated strengthened sounds.

solving

In English, script marks represent sounds pretty loosely:

1

knead	rhythm	thorough
niyd	riðəm	þərow

Nevertheless, for any given word, we can attempt to **solve** the puzzle of which sounds each script mark is supposed to represent:

2

knights	kn	igh	t	s	
	n	ay	t	s	nayts
seeing	s	ee	i	ng	
	s	iy	i	ŋ	siyiŋ

We do this by recognizing patterns. For example, a script mark might be pronounced a certain way at the beginning of a word or when it appears next to certain other script marks, etc:

3

caught	c	au	gh	t	
	k	ho	---	t	khot
phished	ph	i	sh	ed	
	f	i	sy	t	fisyt

The following are only some of the more common ways we solve each script mark.

solving *a*

The script mark *a* is usually pronounced like its equivalent sound mark:

1

bat	*guard*	*math*
bat	gard	maþ

In some words, it is pronounced ha. This usually happens after a p, t or k sound:

2

pat	*tan*	*cab*
phat	than	khab

In some words, it is pronounced ə:

3

apart	*banana*	*capable*
əphart	bənanə	kheypəbəL

This is also usually the case at the end of a word:

4

data	*mocha*	*Russia*
dadə	mowkə	rəsyə

The script marks *ai* and *ay* are usually pronounced ey:

5

fail	*may*	*days*
feyəl	mey	deyəz

In some words, they are pronounced hey. This usually happens after a p, t or k sound:

6

pay	*tail*	*Cayman*
phey	theyL	kheyman

The word *a* is pronounced ey:

7

a cat	*a house*	*a spoon*
eykhat	eyhaws	eyspuwn

However, before a non-whispered open sound, it is written *an* and pronounced an:

8

| *an apple* | *an elephant* | *an honour* |
| anapəL | aneLifənt | anonə |

The script marks *au* and *aw* are usually pronounced o:

9

| *fraud* | *awkward* | *saw* |
| frod | okwərd | so |

In some words, they are pronounced ho. This usually happens after a p, t or k sound:

10

| *paw* | *tawdry* | *cause* |
| pho | thodri | khoz |

solving *b*

The script mark *b* is usually pronounced like its equivalent sound mark:

1

| *beer* | *cab* | *tribe* |
| biyər | kab | trayb |

Two of these script marks next to each other in the same word are usually pronounced as one:

2

| *blubber* | *ebb* | *fibbed* |
| bləbər | eb | fibd |

solving *c*

The script mark *c* has no equivalent sound mark. It is usually pronounced k:

1

| *cat* | *locate* | *McDonald's* |
| khat | lowkheyt | makdOnəldz |

Before the script marks *e* or *i*, it is usually pronounced s:

2

| *center* | *city* | *slicing* |
| senta | siti | slaysiŋ |

Two of these script marks next to each other in the same word are usually pronounced as one:

3

| *accomplish* | *Dacca* | *occur* |
| akhomplisy | daka | OkhəH |

Before the script marks *e* or *i*, they are usually pronounced ks:

4

| *accept* | *accident* | *success* |
| aksept | aksident | səkses |

The script marks *ch* and *tch* are usually pronounced ty:

5

| *chalk* | *China* | *match* |
| tyok | tyayna | maty |

The script marks *ck* are usually pronounced k:

6

| *back* | *chicken* | *neck* |
| bak | tyikin | nek |

solving *d*

The script mark *d* is usually pronounced like its equivalent sound mark:

1

| *date* | *build* | *hurdle* |
| deyʔ | bild | hərdəL |

Two of these script marks next to each other in the same word are usually pronounced as one:

2

| *daddy* | *middle* | *odd* |
| dadi | midəL | od |

The modifier *...ed* that we add to verbs is usually pronounced d:

3

| *described* | *explored* | *stayed* |
| diskraybd | eksplord | steyd |

After a whispered sound, it is pronounced t:

4

| *discussed* | *laughed* | *mapped* |
| diskəst | Laft | mapt |

After a d or t sound, it is pronounced id:

5

| *headed* | *rated* | *waited* |
| hedid | reytid | weytid |

solving *e*

The script mark *e* is usually pronounced like its equivalent sound mark:

1

| *Ben* | *dead* | *yellow* |
| ben | ded | yelow |

In some words, it is pronounced he. This usually happens after a p, t or k sound:

2

| *pen* | *tender* | *kettle* |
| phen | thendər | khedəL |

In some words, it is pronounced ə:

3

beaten	*older*	*present*
biytən	owldər	pɹezənt

At the end of a word, it is usually not pronounced:

4

cake	*dope*	*ridge*
kheyk	dowp	ridy

In this case, any preceding script mark *a* is usually pronounced ey:

5

Dan	*fat*	*mad*
dan	fat	mad

Dane	*fate*	*made*
deyn	feyt	meyd

In some words, it is usually pronounced hey. This usually happens after a p, t or k sound:

6

pan	*tap*	*cam*
phan	thap	kham

pane	*tape*	*came*
pheyn	theyp	kheym

Any preceding script mark *i* is usually pronounced ay:

7

dim	*grim*	*rip*
dim	grim	rip

dime	*grime*	*ripe*
daym	graym	rayp

In some words, it is usually pronounced hay. This usually happens after a p, t or k sound:

8

pin	*Tim*	*kit*
phin	thim	khit

pine	time	kite
phayn	thaym	khayt

Any preceding script mark *o* is usually pronounced ow:

9

mop	nod	rot
mop	nod	rot

mope	node	rote
mowp	nowd	rowt

In some words, it is usually pronounced how. This usually happens after a p, t or k sound:

10

Polly	Tom	cod
pholi	thom	khod

pole	tome	code
phowL	thowm	khowd

Two of these script marks next to each other in the same word are usually pronounced iy:

11

bee	seeing	weed
biy	siyiŋ	wiyd

In some words, they are usually pronounced hiy. This usually happens after a p, t or k sound:

12

peel	tee	keen
phiyəL	thiy	khiyn

This is also the case for the script marks *ea*:

13

eat	sea	tea
iyt	siy	thiy

The script marks *eu*, *ew* and *ue* are usually pronounced either uw or yuw:

eugenics	*few*	*glue*
yuwdyeniks	fyuw	gluw

solving *f*

The script mark *f* is usually pronounced like its equivalent sound mark:

fat	*rifle*	*roof*
fat	Rayfəl	Ruwf

Two of these script marks next to each other in the same word are usually pronounced as one:

coffee	*stuff*	*waffles*
kOfi	stəf	wOfəlz

solving *g*

The script mark *g* is usually pronounced like its equivalent sound mark:

garden	*jog*	*magazine*
gardən	dyog	magəziyn

In some words, the script mark *g* is pronounced dy:

Germany	*gym*	*magic*
dyərməni	dyim	mədyik

This is also the case for the script marks *dg*:

fidget	*ledger*	*smudge*
fidyit	ledyər	smədy

Two of these script marks next to each other in the same word are usually pronounced as one:

| *bigger* | *egg* | *giggle* |
| bigər | eg | gigəL |

At the beginning of a word, the script marks *gu* are usually pronounced g:

| *guardian* | *guide* | *guy* |
| gardiyən | gayd | gay |

This is also the case with the script marks *gh*:

| *ghastly* | *ghetto* | *ghost* |
| gasli | gedow | gowst |

Elsewhere, they are not usually pronounced:

| *daughter* | *sleigh* | *through* |
| dodər | sley | þruw |

However, in some words, they are pronounced f:

| *enough* | *laughs* | *roughage* |
| inəf | Lafs | rəfidy |

The script marks *igh* are usually pronounced ay:

| *fight* | *lighter* | *sigh* |
| fayt | Laydər | say |

solving *h*

The script mark *h* usually indicates that the following open sound is whispered—just like its equivalent sound mark:

1

hedge	his	howl
hedy	hiz	hawəL

However, in some words, it does not indicate this and is not pronounced:

2

exhausted	honest	vehicle
egzostid	onist	viyəkəL

In some words, the script marks *hu* are pronounced ɦuw:

3

hue	Hughes	human
ɦuw	ɦuwz	ɦuwmən

solving *i*

The script mark *i* is usually pronounced like its equivalent sound mark:

1

fit	interest	sing
fit	intrest	siŋ

In some words, it is pronounced hi. This usually happens after a p, t or k sound:

2

pin	tint	king
phin	thint	khiŋ

In some words, it is pronounced ə:

3

Baltimore	pencil	sensitive
bOltəmoH	phensəL	sensətiv

The script marks *io* and *io* are usually pronounced iyow:

4

audio	Neo	videos
odiyow	niyow	vidiyowz

The script marks *ia* and *iu* are usually pronounced iyə:

5

California	Narnia	millennium
kaləfoHniyə	naHniyə	məleniyəm

In some words, the script marks *ind* are usually pronounced aynd:

6

bind	finder	minds
baynd	fayndə	mayndz

solving *j*

The script mark *j* has no equivalent sound mark. It is usually pronounced dy:

1

jam	major	Raj
dyam	meydyə	rAdy

solving *k*

The script mark *k* is usually pronounced like its equivalent sound mark:

2

kite	mark	sneak
khayt	mark	sniyk

At the beginning of a word, the script marks *kn* are usually pronounced n:

3

knee	knife	know
niy	nayf	now

solving *l*

The script mark *l* is usually pronounced like its equivalent sound mark:

1

belt	*Delia*	*look*
beylt	diyliya	luk

In some words, it is pronounced ɫ. This usually happens after a p or k sound:

2

please	*clock*	**play**
pɫiyz	kɫOk	pɫey

Two of these script marks next to each other in the same word are usually pronounced as one:

3

all	*bill*	*million*
al	bil	miliyan

At the end of a word, the script marks *le* are usually pronounced əl:

4

apple	*little*	*riddle*
apəl	likəl	ridəl

solving *m*

The script mark *m* is usually pronounced like its equivalent sound mark:

1

family	*mate*	*zoom*
faməli	meyt	zuwm

Two of these script marks next to each other in the same word are usually pronounced as one:

2

dummy	*mammal*	*slimmer*
dəmi	maməl	slimə

solving *n*

The script mark *n* is usually pronounced like its equivalent sound mark:

1

| *ant* | *nod* | *prisoner* |
| ant | nOd | pɹizəna |

In some words, it is pronounced ŋ. This usually happens before a k sound:

2

| *conquer* | *Hank* | *zinc* |
| khOŋka | haŋk | ziŋk |

In some words, it is pronounced m. This usually happens before a b, p or m sound:

3

| *inbound* | *input* | *government* |
| imbawnd | imput | gOvəment |

Two of these script marks next to each other in the same word are usually pronounced as one:

4

| *Anne* | *channel* | *dinner* |
| an | tyanəw | dina |

The script marks *ng* are usually pronounced ŋ:

5

| *fang* | *ringing* | *strong* |
| faŋ | riŋiŋ | stroŋ |

In some words, they are pronounced ndy:

6

| *binge* | *danger* | *ginger* |
| bindy | deyndya | dyindya |

In some other words, they are pronounced ŋg:

7

| *anger* | *finger* | *tango* |
| aŋga | fiŋga | thaŋgow |

solving *o*

The script mark *o* is usually pronounced like its equivalent sound mark:

1

obstacle	*rotten*	*socks*
obstəkəL	rɔɔən	soks

In some words, it is pronounced ho. This usually happens after a p, t or k sound:

2

pong	*tonsil*	*cog*
phoŋ	thonsəL	khog

In some words, it is pronounced ə:

3

major	*original*	*percolate*
meydyər	əridyənəL	phərkəley?

At the end of a word, it is usually pronounced ow:

4

go	*logo*	*so*
gow	lowgow	sow

Two of these script marks next to each other in the same word are usually pronounced uw:

5

balloon	*goo*	*loop*
bəluwn	guw	luwp

In some words, they are usually pronounced huw. This usually happens after a p, t or k sound:

6

pool	*too*	*cool*
phuwəL	thuw	khuwəL

In some words, they are pronounced u:

7

book	football	wood
buk	fuɔboL	wud

The script marks *oa* and *oe* are usually pronounced ow:

8

goat	Joe	oak
gowt	dyow	owk

In some words, they are usually pronounced how. This usually happens after a p, t or k sound:

9

Poe	toes	coat
phow	thowz	khowt

The script marks *oi* are usually pronounced oy:

10

moist	oil	void
moyst	oyəL	voyd

In some words, they are usually pronounced hoy. This usually happens after a p, t or k sound:

11

poison	toy	coin
phoyzən	thoy	khoyn

solving *p*

The script mark *p* is usually pronounced like its equivalent sound mark:

1

pal	kept	ship
paL	khept	syip

Two of these script marks next to each other in the same word are usually pronounced as one:

2

apple	*happy*	*ripple*
apəL	hapi	ripəL

The script marks *ph* are usually pronounced f:

3

graph	*photo*	*Stephanie*
graf	fowdow	stefəni

At the beginning of a word, the script marks *ps* are usually pronounced s:

4

psalm	*pseudonym*	*psycho*
som	suwdənim	saykow

solving *q*

The script mark *q* has no equivalent sound mark. It usually appears before the script mark *u*. Together, they are pronounced kw or kʌ:

1

equal	*liquid*	*queen*
iykwəL	likwid	kʌiyn

When it doesn't appear before *u*, it is usually pronounced k:

2

Iraq	*Qarth*	*qwerty*
irAk	khaHþ	kʌəHti

solving r

The script mark r is usually pronounced like its equivalent sound mark:

1

bar	boring	rational
bar	boriŋ	rasyənəl

In some words, it is pronounced ɹ. This usually happens after a p, t or k sound:

2

prince	trees	accrue
pɹins	tɹiyz	əkɹuw

Two of these script marks next to each other in the same word are usually pronounced as one:

3

Harry	terrace	worry
hari	therəs	wəri

At the beginning of a word, the script marks rh are usually pronounced r:

4

rhapsody	rhino	rhythm
rapsədi	raynow	riðəm

At the end of a word, the script marks er, or and ure are usually pronounced ər:

5

computer	actor	feature
kəmphuwtər	aktər	fiytyər

The script marks ire are usually pronounced ayər:

6

fire	tired	wires
fayər	thayərd	wayərz

solving *s*

The script mark *s* is usually pronounced like its equivalent sound mark:

1

gas	*sandwich*	*yes*
gas	sanwity	yes

In some words, it is pronounced zy:

2

casual	*measure*	*vision*
khazyuwəL	mezyər	vizyən

In many words, it is pronounced z:

3

business	*is*	*organise*
biznəs	iz	orgənayz

This is also the case with the modifier ...*s* that we add to nouns and verbs and the modifier ...'*s* that we add to nouns:

4

boys	*goes*	*women's*
boyz	gowz	wiminz

After a whispered sound, they are pronounced s:

5

chips	*laughs*	*snake's*
tyips	Lafs	sneyks

After a dy, ty, z, zy, s or sy sound, they are pronounced iz:

6

badges	*fizzes*	*misses*
badyiz	fiziz	misiz
catches	*mirages*	*Ash's*
khatyiz	mirazyiz	asyiz

Two of these script marks next to each other in the same word are usually pronounced as one:

hassle	*miss*	*sassy*
hasəL	mis	sasi

The script marks *sh* are usually pronounced sy:

fashion	*polish*	*shot*
fasyən	pholisy	syot

At the beginning of a word, the script marks *sc* and *sch* are usually pronounced sk:

scandal	*Scott*	*scheme*
skandəL	skot	skiym

solving *t*

The script mark *t* is usually pronounced like its equivalent sound mark:

bat	*hots*	*invest*
bat	hots	invest

Two of these script marks next to each other in the same word are usually pronounced as one:

bottle	*Matt*	*sitting*
botəL	mat	sitiŋ

The script marks *th* are usually pronounced þ:

math	*method*	*three*
maþ	meþəd	þriy

In some words, they are pronounced ð:

4

brother	*then*	*within*
brəðər	ðen	wiðin

This is also the case with the word *the*, which is pronounced ðə:

5

the *door*	**the** *help*	**the** *universe*
ðədor	ðəheLp	ðəyuwnivərs

However, before a non-whispered open sound, it is usually pronounced ðiy:

6

the *ant*	**the** *honest girl*	**the** *umbrella*
ðiyant	ðiyonistgərL	ðiyəmbreLə

The script marks *tion* are usually pronounced syən:

7

alteration	*rendition*	*station*
oLtəreysyən	rendisyən	steysyən

solving *u*

The script mark *u* is only pronounced like its equivalent sound mark in a few words:

1

butcher	*full*	*sugar*
butyə	fuL	syugə

In even fewer words, it is pronounced hu. This usually happens after a p or k sound:

2

pull	*cushion*	*push*
phuL	khusyən	phusy

Otherwise, it is usually pronounced ə:

3

buckle	*mud*	*umbrella*
bəkəL	məd	əmbrelə

In some words, it is pronounced hə. This usually happens after a p, t or k sound:

4

pub	*tumble*	*cub*
phəb	thəmbəL	khəb

In some words, it is pronounced uw:

5

fluke	*Pluto*	*rune*
fluwk	pɾuwtow	ruwn

In other words, it is pronounced yuw:

6

emu	*union*	*universe*
iymyuw	yuwniyən	yuwnəvəHs

solving *v*

The script mark *v* is usually pronounced like its equivalent sound mark:

1

give	*moving*	*veer*
giv	muwviŋ	viyə

solving *w*

The script mark *w* is usually pronounced like its equivalent sound mark:

1

carwash	*shower*	*windy*
kharwosy	syawər	windi

In some words, it is pronounced ʌ. This usually happens after a t sound:

2

between	*twang*	*twinkle*
bitʌiyn	tʌaŋ	tʌiŋkəL

The script marks *wh* are usually pronounced w:

			3
anywhere	*wham*	*white*	
eniwer	wam	wayt	

At the beginning of a word, the script marks *wr* are usually pronounced r:

			4
wrap	*wrench*	*written*	
rap	renty	riɔən	

solving *x*

The script mark *x* has no equivalent sound mark. It is usually pronounced ks:

			1
extreme	*fix*	*Texas*	
ekstriym	fiks	theksəs	

At the beginning of a word, it is usually pronounced z:

			2
Xander	*Xena*	*xenophobic*	
zandər	ziynə	ziynəfowbik	

In some words beginning with the script marks *ex*, it is pronounced gz:

			3
exam	*exit*	*exonerate*	
egzam	egzit	egzonəreyt	

solving *y*

The script mark *y* is usually pronounced like its equivalent sound mark:

			1
buying	*daylight*	*yellow*	
bayiŋ	deylayt	yelow	

At the end of a word, it is usually pronounced i:

2

angry	*lucky*	*nightly*
aŋgri	ləki	naytli

This is also the case with the script marks *ey*:

3

barley	*Harvey*	*money*
barli	harvi	məni

In both cases, it is pronounced iy before another open sound:

4

lucky star	*journey back*	*many people*
ləkistar	dyəHnibak	menipiypəl
lucky apple	*journey on*	*many others*
ləkiyapəl	dyəHniyOn	meniyədəHz

At the end of other words, it is pronounced ay:

5

apply	*cry*	*shy*
əplay	kray	syay

solving z

The script mark z is usually pronounced like its equivalent sound mark:

1

crazy	*organize*	*Zimbabwe*
kɪeyzi	Ogənayz	zimbabwey

Two of these script marks next to each other in the same word are usually pronounced as one:

2

buzz	*fizzle*	*grizzly*
bəz	fizəw	grizli

digitizing

We sometimes say sound marks and script marks individually as separate **digits**—as opposed to the sound or word that those marks represent:

1

The word "key" begins with the sound mark k.
ðəwərdkiy biginzwiðəsawndmark kə

The word "love" contains the script mark v.
ðəwərdLəv kəntheynzðəskriptmark viy

digitizing sound marks

If we need to digitize sound marks, we can refer to those sound marks that represent open sounds by using the open sound itself:

2

a   ə
a   ə

The first open sound of "apple" is represented by the sound mark a.
ðəfərstowpənsawndəvapəL izreprizentidbayðəsawndmark a

The sound mark ə does not have an equivalent script mark.
ðəsawndmark ə dəznothavənikʌivəLəntskriptmark

We can refer to sound marks representing closed sounds by using the closed sound followed by an ə sound:

3

b   bə
g   gə

No, it's with the sound mark b.
now itswiðəsawndmark **bə**

We use the sound mark f to represent a whispered closed sound.
wiyuwzðəsawndmarkfə thəreprizenteiwispərd kɼowzdsawnd

digitizing script marks

When we digitize script marks, we refer to them as follows:

4

a	ey
b	biy
c	siy
d	diy
e	iy
f	ef
g	dyiy
h	eyty
i	ay
j	dyey
k	khey
l	el
m	em
n	en
o	ow
p	phiy
q	kɦuw
r	ar
s	es
t	thiy
u	yuw
v	viy
w	dəbəʟyuw
x	eks
y	way
z	ziy

pitching

We often either lower or raise the **pitch** of our voice at the end of what we are saying:

1

> How are the kids? —Fine.   ↘
> How are the kids? —Fine?   ↗
>
> I have a few suggestions about the department.   ↘
> I have a few suggestions about the department.   ↗

We can pitch over the course of a single word or several words:

2

> Did he call you? —Yes?   ↗
>
> Where you going tonight? —I'm going to Scott's.   ↘

We lower our pitch when we believe that what we are saying is a fact:

3

> Adam's in the diner. (This is a fact.)
> Have you read his new book? —Nope. (No, I haven't.)
> What colour is that? —Blue. (I believe it is blue.)
> What drive thru did you go to? (It's a fact you went to one but tell me which.)
> Jenny didn't make it, did she? (I don't think she did.)

We raise our pitch when we want confirmation that what we are saying is a fact—often because we are surprised:

4

> Adam's in the diner? (This seems to be a fact. I'm surprised. Please confirm.)
> Have you read his new book? —Nope? (Why are you asking me?)

What colour is that? —Blue? (I'm not sure if it's blue. I want you to confirm.)
What drive thru did you go to? (I'm surprised you went to that specific drive thru.)
Jenny didn't make it, did she? (I don't think she did but I want you to confirm.)

We sometimes lower our pitch so much that the voice sounds gravelly and creaky—almost like frying oil:

5

I love this dress... it's so cute.	↘
I love this dress... it's so cute.	↘↘
You just don't get it.	↘
You just don't get it.	↘↘

In this case, we also often spend longer pronouncing what we pitch—so the words are longer and more drawn out:

6

It's definitely painful at the back here.	↘
It's definitely painful at the back here.	↘↘
So the last time we met, we spoke about online trolling.	↘
So the last time we met, we spoke about online trolling.	↘↘

We sometimes raise our pitch even when we don't want confirmation:

7

We were there like... three hours.	↘
We were there like... three hours.	↗↗
When are you moving? —I'm moving February 1st.	↘
When are you moving? —I'm moving February 1st.	↗↗

We often do this in order to come across as less self-assured—and so appear less dominant or threatening to the person we are talking to:

8

OK, put your bags on the table please.	↘
OK, put your bags on the table please.	↗↗
So, let's begin. What's your name?	↘
So, let's begin. What's your name?	↗↗

We also often do this in order to maintain the attention of the person we are talking to—essentially, by constantly asking for clarification:

9

My name is Erica and I come from Long Beach. ↘

My name is Erica and I come from Long Beach. ↗↗

differentiating

We can take a word that has one meaning and recycle it so that it has a different meaning:

1

bluw	did blow
bluw	sad, depressed
bluw	the color blue

The heavy winds **blew** down all the trees.

I've been feeling **blue** all day.

Fill the background with **blue**.

ay	an organ used to see
ay	me, the person speaking

We're just going to shine this light in your **eye**.

I hate going to the dentist.

Often, the only way we can **differentiate** the old word from the new is by context—specifically, the situation we are in or the surrounding words we are using:

2

bakəp	defend
bakəp	make a copy
bakəp	reverse

Why didn't you **back** me up?

I forgot to **back** my work up!

We **backed** the car up into the driveway.

| ðis | one object that is near me in space or time |
| ðis | one object whose identity I will clarify later |

*Why not sit at **this** table?*
*Suddenly, **this** car comes out of nowhere and I had to swerve.*

However, there are certain ways we can differentiate the old word from the new. The following are only some of the more common ways we differentiate by pronunciation.

differentiating by pausing

We can differentiate by pausing. We do this across multiple words:

heard yet	*her jet*
hərdyet	hərdyet
hərd yet	hər dyet
meant use	*men choose*
mentyuwz	mentyuwz
ment yuwz	men tyuwz

3

differentiating by lengthening

We can differentiate by which sound we lengthen:

| biyesiy | a disease affecting cows |
| biyeSiy | an undergraduate degree |

4

*He had to sell his farm after the **BSE** scandal.*
*I have a **BSc** in Engineering.*

| insayt | an understanding |
| insayt | make rebellious |

He was able to gain a few insights.
The preacher incited the crowds.

We often do this with words that would otherwise sound similar—as opposed to exactly the same:

5

k**ho**mit   a passing space rock seen in the sky

kOm**i**t   confirm that you'll do something

The comet was a sign of upcoming doom.
I've already committed to doing 10,000 words.

d**e**zət   a large arid area of land

diz**ə**Ht   sweet food eaten after a main course

It took them several days to cross the desert.
So whaddya want for dessert?

With closed sounds, we usually do this across multiple words as opposed to single words:

6

he earns   *he yearns*

hiyəHnz   hi**y**əHnz

one aim   *one name*

wəneym   wə**n**eym

We also differentiate a small number of words—that are all written with the same script marks—by which open sound we lengthen:

7

kont**e**nt   happy, satisfied

k**ho**ntent   what is contained by something

She was pretty content for a while.
I didn't think much of the content.

eksport   a product that is exported
ekspOrt   send abroad in order to sell

What's the biggest export?
They exported many of their brightest.

flavoring

People from different areas of the planet speak different **flavors** of English:

Did you have anything to eat yet?	Canada
? Did you have anything to eat yet?	Scotland
I've got about 50 lakhs in savings.	India
? I've got about 50 lakhs in savings.	Australia

However, there are very few differences. What differences there are have traditionally been exaggerated in resources—and the remaining differences are rapidly being leveled due to a younger, more universal English-speaking online culture. Likewise, any differences are arguably less significant than with other global languages, such as Portuguese or Spanish:

A gente está comendo uma maçã.	Brazil
Nós estamos a comer uma maçã.	Portugal
We are eating an apple.	Pakistan
We are eating an apple.	South Africa
Vos sos aca.	Argentina
Tu eres aqui.	Spain
You are here.	United States
You are here.	England

The following are only some of the more common ways we flavor pronunciation.

flavoring and sounding

We flavor the following sounds in the following ways.

flavoring the w sound

Many people from Bangladesh, India and Pakistan merge the w sound with the v sound. Here, the top front teeth come close to—but do not touch—the bottom lip. We can represent this with the sound mark V:

1

want	*why*	*hive*
VOnt	Vay	hayV

He's sitting by a wall.
hiyzsiTiŋbayəVol

Some people from England don't pronounce the w sound at all. However, they only do this when the w sound appears between two open sounds:

2

fewer	*going*	*tower*
fyuə	goiŋ	taə

Just lower your standards.
dyəstloəyoHstandədz

flavoring the v sound

As described above, many people from Bangladesh, India and Pakistan merge the w sound with the v sound:

3

version	*nervous*	*alive*
VəHzyən	nəHVəs	əlayV

I voted Conservative.
ayVowTiDkOnsəHVeyTiV

flavoring the ð sound

Many people from Bangladesh, the Caribbean, India, Ireland and Pakistan pronounce the ð sound almost like d:

4

| *then* | *mother* | *with* |
| den | mada | wid |

Then he came back with his brother.
denikheymbakwidizbrəda

Some people from England and the United States pronounce the ð sound like v:

5

| *bothered* | *whether* | *with* |
| bOvəd | wevə | wiv |

Did you see my brother and his wife?
didyəsiymabrəvəanizwayf

flavoring the d sound

Many people from Bangladesh, India and Pakistan pronounce the d sound with the tongue touching a point that is slightly further back towards the roof of the mouth. We can represent this with the sound mark D:

6

| *David* | *medium* | *mad* |
| DeyViD | miyDiyəm | maD |

Dana likes dancing.
DeynəlayksDAnsiŋ

flavoring the l sound

Many people from Australia, Canada, New Zealand, Scotland and the United States pronounce the l sound with the back of the tongue moving toward the back of the throat. We can represent this with the sound mark L:

7

Larry	*fills*	*well*
Lari	fiLz	weL

She loved him well enough.
syiLəvdhimweLinəf

Many people from England and South Africa also do this. However, they don't usually do this before an open sound:

8

lime	*melt*	*pal*
laym	meLt	paL

Look at that lovely field.
lukəʔðaɔləvlifiyəLd

Some people from Australia, England, New Zealand, the United States and West Africa pronounce the l sound like w. They don't do this before an open sound:

9

lemon	*golf*	*till*
lemən	gOwf	thiw

I'm breathing in the chemicals.
ambriyviŋinðəkhemikəwz

In both cases, when the l sound comes to be followed by an open sound, it reverts back to normal:

10

It was hell!
iʔwOzheL

It was hell in there!
iʔwOzhelinðeH

I need a bottle.
ayniydəbOɔƏw

I need a bottle of milk.
ayniydəbOtələvmiLk

flavoring the r sound

Many people from Australia, Bangladesh, England, India, New Zealand, Pakistan, South Africa and Wales don't pronounce the r sound at all. However, they don't do this before an open sound:

11

Richard	*carrier*	*later*
rityəd	khariə	leytə

He looks younger.
hiluksyəŋgə

This causes the previous open sound to be pronounced longer. We can represent this by adding the mark H after the open sound:

12

learn	*March*	*for*
ləHn	maHty	foH

Let it burn.
letiɔbəHn

At the end of a word, the ə sound is not usually pronounced longer:

13

matter	*nature*	*wider*
matə	neytyə	waydə

Cya later!
siyəleytə

Many people from the Caribbean and West Africa—and some people from England and South Africa—pronounce this ə almost as a:

14

data
deyəta

mocha
mowəka

Russia
rəsya

The soldier jumped down from the helicopter.
ðəsowldyadyumpdownfrOmdielikOpta

When the r sound comes to be followed by an open sound, the r sound reverts back to normal (though people from South Africa don't usually do this):

15

She seems older when I look at this picture.
syisiymzOLdəwenaylukəɔðispiktyə

She seems older in this picture of Anne's.
syisiymzOLdərinðispiktyərəvanz

Many people from Australia, Bangladesh, England, India, New Zealand, Pakistan and Wales (but not South Africa) insert a r sound when an open sound comes to be followed by an unwhispered open sound:

16

America and Britain
əmerikərənbritən

Mocha or cappuccino?
mOkəroHkapətyiynow

Many people from Bangladesh, India, Pakistan, Scotland and South Africa pronounce the r sound with the tongue tapping against the flat area above the ridge above the top teeth. We can represent this with the sound mark R:

17

ring
Riŋ

foreign
foRin

Gerry
dyeRi

I'm rich.
aymrity

flavoring the y sound

Some people from England don't pronounce the y sound at all. However, they only do this between two open sounds:

18

fire	hear	playing
faə	hiə	pɾeiŋ

Stop toying with him.
stOpthoiŋwiðhim

flavoring open sounds

Some people from Australia, Bangladesh, England, India, New Zealand, Pakistan, South Africa and West Africa pronounce the a sound longer than normal in certain words. We can represent this with the sound mark A:

19

gas	ant	math
gas	ant	maþ

pass	aunt	bath
phAs	Ant	bAþ

Many people from the Caribbean and West Africa avoid using the ə sound. Instead, they use an alternative sound suggested by the script mark:

20

banana	pencil	original
bənanə	phensəL	əridyənəL

banana	pencil	original
banana	phensil	oridyinal

Many people from Australia, Bangladesh, England, India, New Zealand, Pakistan, South Africa and West Africa pronounce the o sound shorter than normal in certain words. We can represent this with the sound mark O:

21

cot	collar	hock
khOt	khOlə	hOk

caught	*caller*	*hawk*
khot	kholə	hok

flavoring and whispering

We flavor the following whispered sounds in the following ways.

flavoring the þ sound

Many people from Bangladesh, the Caribbean, India, Ireland and Pakistan pronounce the þ sound almost like t:

22

thin	*mathematics*	*death*
thin	matəmatiks	det

I think he's too thin.
aythiŋkiyzthuwthin

Some people from England, South Africa and the United States pronounce the þ sound like f:

23

thank	*method*	*math*
faŋk	mefəd	maf

I think I'll be thin enough.
ayfiŋkawbifininəf

flavoring the t sound

Many people from Australia, Canada, New Zealand and the United States pronounce the t sound like d. However, they only do this when the t sound appears between two open sounds or between a w or y sound and an open sound:

24

Get a little bit.
gedəLidəLbiʔ

I'll go to him later.
aʟgowdəhimʟeydə

Get outta here!
gedɑwdəhiyə

Many people from Bangladesh, India and Pakistan pronounce the t sound with the tongue touching a point that is slightly further back towards the roof of the mouth. We can represent this sound with the sound mark ⊤:

25

time	*matter*	*hate*
⊤aym	ma⊤ə	hey⊤

Can you turn the temperature up?
kanyuw⊤əHnðə⊤emprə⊤ərəp

flavoring the ɾ sound

Many people from Australia, Canada, New Zealand, Scotland and the United States flavor the ɾ sound the same way they flavor the l sound. Again, the back of the tongue moves toward the back of the throat. We can represent this sound with the sound mark ɼ:

26

plenty	*clear*	*reply*
pɼenti	kɼiyə	ripɼay

So what's the plan?
sowOtsðəpɼan

flavoring the ɹ sound

Many people from Scotland and South Africa flavor the ɹ sound the same way they flavor the r sound. Again, the tongue taps against the flat area above the ridge above the top teeth. We can represent this sound with the sound mark я:

27

tree	*prince*	*cry*
tяiy	pяins	kяay

Don't even try to call me.
downtiyvəntЯaytəkhoʟmiy

flavoring whispered open sounds

Some people from Australia, the Caribbean and England don't whisper open sounds:

hat	*home*	*high*
at	owəm	ay

This is my home.
disizmayowəm

Many people from Bangladesh, India, Pakistan and South Africa don't whisper an open sound after a p, t or k sound:

pin	*tumble*	*king*
pin	təmbəl	kiŋ

Take Peter to the car please.
teykpiytətəðəkarpliyz

flavoring and solving

Some people from England and the United States pronounce the modifier *...ing* that we add to verbs as in:

going	*saying*	*singing*
gowin	seyin	siŋin

What are you saying?
wOdəyuwseyin

Some people from Ireland, Scotland and the southern United States pronounce the script marks wh as a whispered w sound. We can represent this by putting the sound mark h before w:

wine	which	what
weyn	hwity	hwOt

Why did he say that?
hwaydidiseyðat?

flavoring and digitizing

People from outside the United States usually digitize the script mark z as zed:

32

The word zoo begins with Z.
ðəwərdzuw biginzwiðziy

The word zoo begins with Z.
ðəwəHdzuw biginzwiðzed

flavoring and pitching

Lowering our pitch so much that the voice sounds gravelly and creaky—almost like frying oil—is particularly common in the United States, especially among younger women:

I just hate that color.	↘
I just hate that color.	↘↘
We flew back to Los Angeles last Thursday.	↘
We flew back to Los Angeles last Thursday.	↘↘

Raising our pitch even when we don't want confirmation is particularly common in Australia, New Zealand and some parts of the United States:

34

Well, I'd like to eventually move into finance. ↘

Well, I'd like to eventually move into finance. ↗↗

We'd definitely have to come up with a schedule. ↘

We'd definitely have to come up with a schedule. ↗↗

bleaching

For any given language, we can use that language in a way that indicates we have a higher social status, education or level of prestige:

1

> *Power is power.*
> phawə izphawə
> phaə izphaə   higher prestige

> *We need alot of bread if your going to the store.*
> *We need **a lot** of bread if you're going to the store.*   higher prestige

In English, this mainly involves us not using certain features of the language—as opposed to introducing anything significantly new. In other words, we **bleach** the language of certain features:

2

> * *I would of called you but you never answer!*
> *I would **have** called you but you never answer!*   bleached

> * *It's different to what we're used to.*
> *It's different **from** what we're used to.*   bleached

Bleaching is therefore just another flavor—but one based on social status rather than geography:

3

> *And the Chaser will offer you... thirty thousand pounds!*
> * anðətyeysəwilOfəyuw   fəHtifawzəndphawndz
> anðətyeysəwilOfəyuw   þəHtiþawzəndphawndz

> * *No, you'll be sat next to your sister.*
> *No, you'll be **sitting** next to your sister.*

Because they have not been used by people of higher social status, many of the features we bleach have historically been considered "incorrect"—despite being used by huge numbers of people. Even now, you will still find them presented as "incorrect" in almost all contemporary resources that teach English:

4

> * There are less reasons now to do that.
> There are **fewer** reasons now to do that.
>
> * Lets go to Davids.
> **Let's** go to **David's**.

The following are only some of the more common ways we bleach pronunciation.

bleaching and weakening

When we bleach, we tend to weaken less:

5

> Put it on the computer.
> * phuɔɔciOnðəkəmpyuwɔə
> ? phuɔɔciOnðəkəmpyuwtə
> phutiɔOnðəkəmpyuwtə
> phutit Onðəkəmpyuwtə
>
> Here are your things.
> * iyərəyəþiŋz
> hiyərəyəþiŋz
> hiyəraHyoHþiŋz

bleaching and flavoring

When we bleach, those people from England who don't pronounce the w sound at all between two open sounds tend to do this more when they bleach:

6

fewer	going	tower
? fyuwə	? gowiŋ	? thawə
fyuə	goiŋ	thaə

Those people from England and the United States who pronounce the ð sound like v tend to do this less when they bleach:

7

bothered	whether	with
? bOvəd	? wevə	? wiv
bOðəd	weðə	wið

Those people from Australia, England, New Zealand, the United States and West Africa who pronounce the l sound like w tend to do this less when they bleach:

8

lemon	golf	till
lemən	? gOwf	? thiw
lemən	gOlf	thil

Those people from England who don't pronounce the ɹ sound at all between two open sounds tend to do this more when they bleach:

9

hear	fire	playing
? hiɹə	? faɹə	? pɹeyiŋ
hiə	faə	pɹeiŋ

Those people from South Africa who pronounce the r sound with the tongue tapping against the flat area above the ridge above the top teeth tend to do this less when they bleach:

10

Peter	regular	tomorrow
? piytəR	? RegyələR	? təmORow
piytə	regyələ	təmOrow

Those people from England, South Africa and the United States who pronounce the þ sound like f tend to do this less when they bleach:

11

thank	method	math
? faŋk	? mefəd	? maf
þaŋk	meþəd	maþ

Those people from Australia, the Caribbean and England who don't whisper open sounds tend to do this less when they bleach:

12

hat	*home*	*hype*
? at	? owəm	? ayp
hat	howm	hayp

Those people from Ireland, Scotland and the southern United States who pronounce the script marks *wh* as a whispered *w* sound tend to do this more when they bleach:

13

well	*when*	*why*
weL	? wen	? way
weL	hwen	hway